Also by Peri Wolfman and Charles Gold

Great Settings

Forks, Knives & Spoons

Birdhousing

The Perfect Setting

A Place for Everything

Organizing the Stuff of Life

Peri Wolfman and Charles Gold

Photographs by Charles Gold

Clarkson Potter/Publishers
New York

To Daisy, Gertrude, and Rose, who constantly foil our efforts for neatness and order. That's life!

Copyright © 1999 by Peri Wolfman and Charles Gold

All rights reserved. No part of this book may be reproduced or transmitted in any form or by any means, electronic or mechanical, including photocopying, recording, or by any information storage and retrieval system, without permission in writing from the publisher.

Published by Clarkson Potter/Publishers, 201 East 50th Street, New York, New York 10022. Member of the Crown Publishing Group.

Random House, Inc. New York, Toronto, London, Sydney, Auckland
www.randomhouse.com

CLARKSON N. POTTER, POTTER, and colophon are registered trademarks of Random House, Inc.

Printed in China

Design by Richard Ferretti

Library of Congress Cataloging-in-Publication Data
Wolfman, Peri.
A place for everything : organizing the stuff of life / Peri Wolfman and Charles Gold ;
photographs by Charles Gold.
p.   cm.
1. Storage in the home. I. Gold, Charles. II. Title.
TX309.W65   1999
648'.8—DC21   98-55420
                                                CIP

ISBN 0-609-80448-0 (paperback)
ISBN 0-609-50286-7 (hardcover)

10   9   8   7   6   5   4   3   2   1

First Edition

Acknowledgments

Thanks to all of our friends who first said no, but then cautiously opened the doors of their closets, allowing us to snoop and photograph in their private domain.

Peter Biskind
Larry Bogdanow
Stephen Brady
Bobbi Brown
Kathe and Reid Chase
Chuck and Leslie Close
Brian Colwell and Vikki Leftwich
Richard Crisman and Jeffrey Brock
Joel Dean and Jack Ceglic
Pat and Allan Dennis
Michele Oka Doner
Liza and David Freilicher
Stanlee Gatti
Elizabeth Gerschell
Jeff McKay
Robert Lee Morris
Claudia Schwarts and Toby Hanson
Patrick Wade and Dave Di Matte
Laura and Alexander Wolfman

A very special thank-you to:

Roy Finamore, a great editor and collaborator and an outstanding folder.

Richard Ferretti, who is not only the most talented designer but also the neatest!

Randi Halpern, for whipping up all of those handy diagrams.

Contents

A collection of unmatched brass candlesticks is gathered to fill the tabletop and illuminate an eighteenth-century portrait.

Introduction

When I was a little girl, maybe nine or ten years old, my mother unwittingly taught me a lesson of neatness that has been with me ever since. She didn't fancy herself a housekeeper, and I know she didn't define her role in life as constantly cleaning up after her three messy little girls. But I also have no memory of our mother ever nagging us, telling us to put our clothes away, although I'm sure she had!

My sister Laurie and I shared a room with two matching closets that were separated by a dresser built under a large window. The dresser had an equal number of drawers for each of us.

We never used the closets or the dresser. Instead, every night when we changed into our pajamas, Laurie would drop her clothes on the floor of her closet. I neatly folded mine and put them on a chintz-covered armchair next to my closet. Even then I liked the idea of being able to see all of my clothes at a glance. The piles grew taller. My recollection is that when we needed something to wear, we just took it from the bottom, middle, or top of our respective piles.

Our mother, however, didn't distinguish between Laurie's mountains of rumpled sweaters or sundresses and my very neatly folded pile of things. One day when we arrived home from school, we found our room looking like a tornado had swept through. Clothes were everywhere—on top of our bed canopies, under the beds, on the lamp shades, on the desk. Almost everything we owned—my sister's heaps and my month's worth of carefully folded and piled clothes—was strewn about. It was a very strong message for me: neatness counts!

That afternoon when we discovered the devastation, our mother was nowhere around, but the message was clear. We folded, hung, and put everything where it belonged without any argument.

I became a world-class clothes folder long before Gap-style folding became a world-renowned art. My stacks of folded clothes on the chair marked the beginning of my preference for open storage, where everything is visible, instead of the throw-it-in-the-closet-and-shut-the-door school.

As I grew up and had my own homes, accumulating more rooms with more

An aged galvanized commercial
flower bucket makes an ideal
container for umbrellas.

stuff, raising boy children and an assortment of dogs, cats, and doves, the art of being neat became more complicated. It was a real-life challenge for which I was always looking for answers.

I was forever rethinking the best way to control kid clutter. There were no simple solutions, but there were some sensible concepts for organization and storage that worked then and still work for me today.

One was the use of baskets. Lots of matching, medium-size baskets work best, whether they are wicker, wood, or plastic. My theory is that if the containers are all the same the clutter looks organized. If the baskets are not too big and the kids can see what's in them, they won't have to go digging everything out.

Here's a tip: Always buy more containers than you think you need today, because tomorrow the stuff will expand and you'll wish you had more, and of course you won't be able to find them ever again.

The other old standby is installing rows of hooks or pegs in strategic places, within the reach of little children's arms. It's much easier for children to hang their coats on hooks than to hang their clothes on hangers. And when the kids don't comply with your "Be Neat" rules, which is likely, you can quickly get the clothes off the floor and onto a hook. This is also a solution that works well in guest rooms where closets are scarce.

As is the nature of things, our boys grew up. The last one has just moved into his own apartment. He has almost emptied out his closets in our home. We have all survived those rough-and-tumble years, each with his or her own sensibility. Now that I no longer have the excuse of kids, little or big, messing things up, I can indulge my innate instinct to keep order, but it is still a challenge. There is so much stuff to deal with in our everyday lives: mail, magazines and newspapers, toiletries, in- and out-of-season clothes, recyclables, photographs, and memorabilia. I keep thinking that there is some trick, some secret to order that someone else knows, and I'm just dying to be let in on it.

There's something about a closed door that stimulates curiosity. Most of us would like to peek behind the closed doors in the homes of our most stylish friends and acquaintances, especially if they appear to possess the keys to being very neat and organized.

What better way to uncover secrets than to be a journalist, a style snoop, an authority on neatness, and to write a book on closets, storage, and clutter control? So I outlined a book on storage and got to work looking for neat-freaks with great closets. But anytime I told friends that Charley and I were producing a book on closets and would like to photograph theirs, a frightened look came over their faces. And I heard every excuse! "No, no, we have no closets." "We're moving tomorrow." "We're in the middle of a major renovation."

So I changed my approach. I simply said we were working on a book about storage, arranging collections, and how people organize their stuff. Then they started to listen; some even said they had an idea or two. Most let us take a look. Once we were in the door we found original, personal, and creative solutions to storage, dozens of intelligent and stylish ideas for coping with all the possessions we seem to amass in our modern lives.

Even the most mundane "stuff" can be creatively arranged. Necklaces dangle from pegs in a bathroom; coats and hats hang on hooks in the front entry; towels are rolled in a big wicker basket. Old painted benches stacked up become shelving for books and magazines, things that would be clutter if left unorganized. We learned that by arranging items in groups by color, shape, or function on well-thought-out shelves or in great old cabinets or in baskets, they take on the aura of a well-maintained collection instead of a hodgepodge.

Unfortunately, being organized is not a onetime fix. Like a garden, a closet requires regular tending and care. It won't keep itself in order. If you're going to have a neat, orderly, and beautiful garden in the spring, you will need to clean up and weed out old plants in the fall. It's the same with your clothes closet, dish shelves, collection of photographs, and files—they take regular tending to stay untangled and looking their best.

Closets are a relatively recent innovation. Before the late nineteenth century, all household possessions were kept in freestanding cupboards, cabinets, wardrobes, armoires, and linen presses, or on hooks and shelves. Houses constructed before 1900 had no clothes closets, though there was the occasional china closet built into the dining room.

In the 1920s boxlike closets appeared in the corners of bedrooms; although convenient, they gave the room an awkward shape. In the forties and fifties it became fashionable to use "modern" bifold doors on long narrow closets built along one

wall of a bedroom. A version of this simple solution for allocating space to storage has continued today. No matter what shape a closet assumes, it takes space from a room; therefore, building a closet is not just about storage but also about the architecture of the room. Throughout this book, we have tried to show pleasing ways to add closet space, whether in the form of a built-in closet or a piece of free-standing furniture.

Our opinion that it is not always necessary to resort to expensive built-in closets for storage is reinforced by not only history but also personal style and preference. We find that a freestanding cupboard adds a handsome architectural element to a room, takes up the same amount of space as a built-in but doesn't close in the room visually, and isn't as costly. The process of installing it doesn't disrupt your life as much as building a closet, and you can take furniture with you when you move.

In the kitchen, we have a preference for open shelving. Open shelves make the room visually larger than do traditional overhead cabinets. Because they let you see all of your china and glassware, you won't forget anything stored in a dark corner. And chances are, if you can see it, you'll use it. That leads us to another important tip about storage: If you haven't been using something and it seems likely that you won't, get rid of it!

Our intention in photographing and writing *A Place for Everything* was to offer lots of solutions to everyday problems of keeping up with things that accumulate. Charley and I don't really believe that being neat and organized means your life will be perfect. We do think that simply being able to find a safety pin when you need it or your favorite sweater when you're dressing for work, or having a place to toss the mail each night and a consistent spot to keep the magazines you want to look at again, can make your life less stressful.

If you are as interested as we are in the ways different people have organized the accumulated paraphernalia in their lives, then turn the pages of this book. We hope you will discover the ultimate answer to a clutter-free life, but short of that dream, at least a life filled with artfully and creatively arranged stuff!

The space under the staircase
was claimed for storage by
building a wall with a door.

CHAPTER I

The "Everything" Closet

Closet a secret or private place

Laundry a place where clothes are washed and pressed

Wardrobe a room for containing clothes

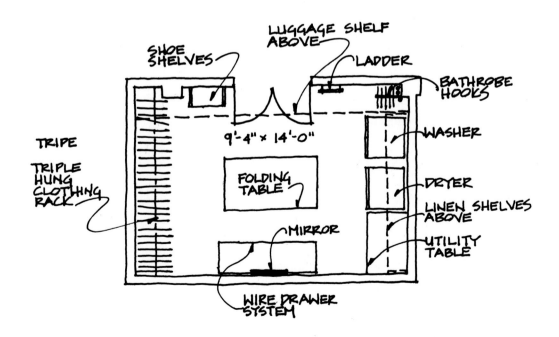

Most people dream of a lofty living room. I dreamed of a lofty closet. In our New York City loft, behind a pair of French doors, next to our bedroom and across from the bath, there is a room where we have closeted all of our storage needs. It is a very private place, big enough to walk around in, big enough to dress in, just big enough to contain all its uses. Linen closet, clothes closet, and laundry room—all in one! Long ago I came to the conclusion that laundry rooms belonged upstairs, near the linen and bedroom closets. Why carry all that stuff up and down stairs? From there, it was a quick leap to the notion of doing it all in the same room. So here in my "everything" closet, soiled clothes and linens are thrown into hampers. Here they are laundered, pressed, and folded. And here they end up on shelves, in baskets, on hangers.

Not every home offers the luxury of an extra room to devote to such a closet. However, if you are willing to give up the notion of a large bedroom with clothes closets and dressers, you can devote the saved space to closeting everything in a room of its own. When we made the trade-off, our bedroom became exactly that, a bedroom—a place for sleeping, reading, and listening to music.

PAGE 14, TOP: The bare bones. We started by setting up a bank of wire shelves that could contain all of our folded clothes. The shelf across the top of the unit not only provides additional storage but also makes the system much sturdier.

PAGE 14, BOTTOM: The closet filled. An old enamel-topped table becomes the ideal surface for folding clothes. The basket under it hides garment and tote bags (suitcases are on high shelves), so even our packing needs are in the same room. There are two laundry baskets: one is for washing (left), and the other is for ironing.

TOP: The shelf above the door is just wide enough to keep suitcases up and out of the way.

LEFT: The shoe cubbies were built to fit the length of my shoes so I can easily see each pair.

Because of the weight of the Marseilles spreads I collect and use throughout the house, the shelves and brackets needed to be extra sturdy.

TIP **All linens are heavy, so make sure your brackets are sturdy and closely spaced to prevent shelves from bowing.**

The table with shelves next to the dryer holds a panoply of supplies. The glass jar contains laundry detergent. Baskets hide shoe-cleaning, dog-grooming, and other supplies.

We are fortunate to have ceilings that are high enough to allow triple-hung storage. Trousers and skirts hang on the bottom pole, shirts and jackets on the middle, and out-of-season garments on top, with shoulder protectors to avoid dust damage.

The shelf atop the center section of the wall unit doubles as a dressing table—a home to my collections of vintage pins, mementos, and spectacles.

Paper, Pencils, and Pens

Computers were supposed to free us of paper and the need to file!
That didn't happen. Now our home offices not only have
stacks of papers and filing systems but are stuffed with office supplies
and, of course, the computer, keyboard, and printer. The challenge is to find a neat
and organized method for keeping our home office still looking like part of our home.

1 The office, disorganized. At the end of my long, narrow home office is an antique pine cupboard that I use to store paper and stationery.

2 "Laundry" baskets in the organized office are retrofitted with hanging file frames. The same laundry baskets work well to contain reference books. Sturdy canvas bags, which are just the right size for file folders, are a necessity for projects that need to go from place to place with me.

TIP Using antique and vintage furniture for your home office will give it a softer, less institutional look and feel, but task lighting is a must.

3 Paper, pencils, staplers, and tape often rattle in drawers or clutter the work surface. Like puzzle pieces, these odds and ends await being fitted into the toolbox.

4 Frames for hanging files are available in office supply stores. These sturdy baskets from Basketville are the ideal size (see Resources, page 187).

5 The vintage toolbox keeps office necessities handy and tidy.

6 A barrister's bookcase can easily be converted into a home for correspondence cards, labels, and other stationery.

7 If you must have file cabinets in your living space, make them an architectural statement.

TIP The steps formed by the files are an ideal place for showing off a collection or art.

CHAPTER II

Kitchens and Dining Rooms

Cupboard a place for keeping victuals, dishes, etc.

Cutlery Drawer a thing drawn out, such as the sliding box in a chest

Pantry a room or closet for provisions and table furnishings

Pots and pans, dishes and platters, cooking and dining utensils, produce and dry goods: no other room in the house is expected to house such a large and varied assortment of everyday needs and just plain stuff. Even though kitchens come with cabinets and drawers, they usually fall short of our needs! The trick is to discover ways to supplement existing storage space without resorting to the extremes of renovation.

The first step toward additional storage is to look for unused space. Add simple open shelves over windows or doors to house a collection of bowls or pitchers that aren't used every day. Install wire or glass shelves in deep windows to create a great showplace for collections of clear or colored glass that catch the light.

Kitchen storage doesn't have to be the typical built-in overhead or under-counter cabinet. Antique cabinets, jelly cupboards, open shelving, even iron pot stands can add a practical yet quirky element to the storage needs of any kitchen.

Organization may be the most important consideration. Taking the time to retrofit a drawer to your particular collection of cutlery, transferring dry goods to clear containers in the pantry, and putting all of the clutter in your junk drawer in a premade divider will save you from frustrating, frantic searching.

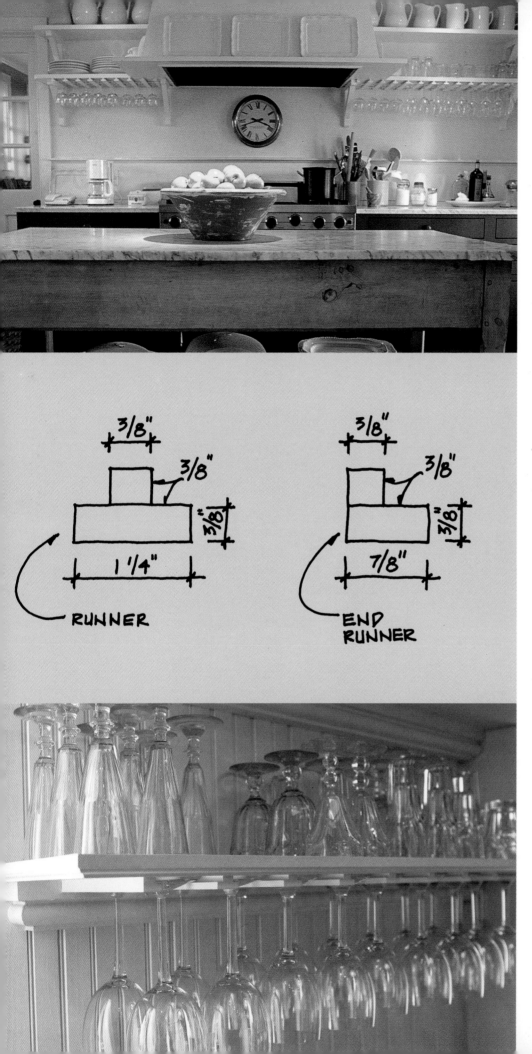

RUNNER

END RUNNER

27

PRECEDING PAGES: These open shelves hold a collection of white kitchen porcelain (see also pages 38–39).

Designed to show off collections of white ironstone and glass, open shelves also make this kitchen appear more spacious and airy than it would with typical overhead cabinets.

The top shelves house ironstone jugs that are used only occasionally. Dinnerware stacked on the lower shelves is easy to reach; stemmed glasses hang underneath.

TIP By hanging stemmed glasses under a shelf, you can double your storage capacity.

The glass hangers are made by screwing wooden runners into the underside of the shelf. Measure the distance between the runners by using the base of the stemmed glass you plan to hang; be sure to check the base of each different type of glass for size. Mark the location of each runner on the underside of the shelf. Paint the runners to match the shelf, then screw them into the bottom of the shelf (see also page 43).

A shelf for large serving bowls and platters has been created by suspending a piece of ¾-inch Plexiglas on the stretchers of this eighteenth-century French baker's table.

When there is space between the top of a window frame and the ceiling (even 10 or 12 inches is enough), you can easily install a shelf with wood brackets. It becomes an attractive place for housing a collection.

There is nothing kitcheny in the SoHo loft of artist Michele Oka Doner, where the artist's eye is always evident yet the solutions are practical and usable. Oka Doner found storage space by treating the huge windows that run the length of the entire kitchen wall as recesses. By screwing metro shelving into the window frames, she left the vintage moldings undamaged and intact.

TIP Wire shelving in a window almost disappears and allows the daylight to shine in.

Gandhi the parrot has the run of the loft but always flies back to his perch, a shelf that floats above the sill in the deep, sun-filled window.

A magnetic knife bar is mounted prominently, creating an almost sculptural effect. Nothing could be handier.

OPPOSITE: Metro shelving screwed into the window frame requires no complicated carpentry.

S hooks are used to hang tiny pots, cups, and kitchen collectibles.

Oka Doner designed and cast the sterling silver platters that sparkle in the deep, tall windows.

In the SoHo loft of Joel Dean and Jack Ceglic, cofounders of the renowned food emporium Dean & DeLuca, stands a bank of vertical file cabinets. These are no ordinary files—this is kitchen storage. The front panels slide up like garage doors; the open drawers then pull out to reveal a collection of teapots or buffet plates or other kitchen items.

Narrow map drawers lined in Pacific cloth are a clever solution for storing silver cutlery.

Antique or new iron pot stands add an interesting architectural quality to a kitchen or dining room. They take up very little floor space and can be used to hold stacks of china.

Jack Ceglic had a great idea for safely storing a collection of potter Barbara Eigen's square buffet plates. A piece of sheet metal was bent to match the corner of the plates and welded to a flat bottom square of stainless steel on which the plates sit. The collection is out of the way yet still visible under the open kitchen counter.

The open shelves in this airy kitchen are suspended from the ceiling instead of being attached to the walls. Plumbing pipe (PVC) and flange fittings replace more conventional bracket shelf supports. The stainless-steel table—ordered from a professional restaurant equipment supplier—was made with two additional shelves for storage of large serving pieces.

PRECEDING PAGES AND RIGHT: A shelf built with step-back ogee molding is supported by a 1 × 3-inch board; the chunky molding under that is decorative. To double the usable space, tumblers are stacked on top of the shelf and stemmed glasses are hung on wood hangers under the shelf.

Give yourself more work space by getting the canisters off the counter—just build a short shelf in an easy-to-reach place. Glass canisters allow you to see what you have on hand; you can buy them at housewares stores.

TIP **You can find replacement knobs for the chrome lids of glass canisters at hardware stores. Change the knobs of these canisters from their original red to white porcelain, or choose any knob you like.**

The wood plate rack is a reproduction of an English antique.

TIP **In Italy, plate and platter racks have slatted, open bottoms and are often hung over the kitchen sink where washed dishes drain, air-dry, and are stored.**

OPPOSITE: Glass storage, maximized.

Refrigerators are the bulkiest appliance in any kitchen, and building them in often means just another big box. The solution here incorporates the refrigerator into an entire wall with floor-to-almost-ceiling closets on either side. Wide crown molding ties it all together both visually and structurally. You can see into the pantry and china closet, but not too clearly, through a matched set of old French doors that are newly fitted with a double layer of copper screening.

TIP **You can buy premade screen doors at lumberyards, or look for vintage screen doors at outdoor summer antique shows. Replace the old screen with a double layer of copper or other metal screening to create a moiré effect.**

A glass-front restaurant refrigerator is a handsome appliance, but it's only for serious, neat cooks. Bunches of herbs look great in this refrigerator, but old chocolate cakes and containers of takeout don't belong here.

If you are building or renovating your kitchen, you'll probably find the refrigerator is the most difficult appliance to fit in gracefully. In this country kitchen, the appliance is concealed as a cupboard in the corner of the room. The "fridge" label was added when guests couldn't figure out that it in fact *was* a refrigerator.

TIP When buying a new refrigerator, look at the slim built-ins that have the option of custom front-panel kits.

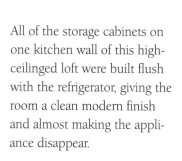

All of the storage cabinets on one kitchen wall of this high-ceilinged loft were built flush with the refrigerator, giving the room a clean modern finish and almost making the appliance disappear.

OPPOSITE: Shelves from an old butcher shop, with their peeling paint intact, were found at a flea market and simply screwed into the walls of this pantry. The walls were painted a shade of green to enhance rather than match the shelves. Collected kitchen paraphernalia looks great against the odd greens.

TIP Be on the lookout for odd shelves, or brackets to hold new shelves, at flea markets and antique shows. They are usually less expensive than custom brackets and give you instant gratification.

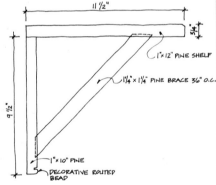

11 1/2"
3/4"
1"x 12" PINE SHELF
1 1/4" x 1 1/4" PINE BRACE 36" O.C.
9 1/2"
1"x10" PINE
DECORATIVE ROUTED BEAD

Oversize wood brackets similar to shelf brackets support a tabletop. There's plenty of room left underneath for recycling baskets of flat woven New England ash.

TIP To give the baskets a finished look, as if they were part of the room, paint the outsides to match the walls. Keep the insides natural for better wear.

The pantry in the home of a busy young family has everything at hand to create multiple meals. Clear containers protect staples from moisture and bugs.

You can protect food and see what you need to replace by storing staples in clear glass jars. Rural tag sales and antique markets are great sources for old preserving jars.

TIP Housewares and hardware stores sell replacement rubber gaskets for old jars as well as new glass preserving jars.

A neat and simple way to build sturdy wood shelves that support the weight of heavy china is to run wood molding under the entire length and width of each shelf.

TIP Using a screen door instead of a solid panel door on your pantry or china closet allows air to circulate and prevents the pantry from getting musty.

The littlest kitchen of all is literally concealed behind closed doors. Perfect for urban adman Jeff McKay, who eats out almost every night, it has all the basics for morning coffee and evening cocktails.

You may think that the greater the shelf area in a small closet, the better you can store groceries and staples. Not so. In this little closet, viewing supplies is made easier and more efficient by shelves cut in a U shape rather than deep, straight-across rows.

Shelves for spice jars are made of the same wood as the door and precisely notched out so the jars won't come crashing down every time the door is opened.

TIP Use the door for added shelf space. You can buy ready-made shelving that is designed to be installed on pantry doors.

Medical test tubes in their rack make neat, visible, and handsome containers for spices.

Even in a spacious closet, narrow shelves make for better pantry storage than wide shelves—there's no reaching behind things. The stack of twenty-four buffet plates, too heavy for any shelf, sits comfortably on the floor until the next party.

TIP Make use of floor space for heavy nonfood items.

A very wide, shallow kitchen drawer is laid out like a jigsaw puzzle. Everything is fitted tightly, which prevents sliding around even without dividers. The double-tier organizer keeps all of the little clutter in place.

A deep lower kitchen drawer is dedicated to baking paraphernalia.

TIP If you are building or renovating a kitchen, consider installing large drawers instead of cabinets under the counter. And try to categorize items in drawers by their use.

OPPOSITE: The kitchen side of a counter that divides dining and cooking space can be practical and utilitarian. The compactor, microwave, and drawers are built in. Cut-out "garage" spaces open to the floor and house the trash basket, recycling bins, cutting boards, and platters.

TIP When planning a kitchen renovation, be sure to allocate space for recycling containers.

When complete renovation isn't an option, retrofit under-counter cabinets to become recycling drawers.

If your kitchen isn't blessed with lots of drawer space, display your flatware and cooking utensils in great-looking containers. An old country toolbox divided into sections is ideal for forks, knives, and spoons.

This wooden toolbox serves as a tray for assorted condiments.

TIP When setting the table for dinner, you can carry the toolbox with all of the condiments in just one trip.

A collection of bone- and wood-handled dinner knives from the turn of the century looks great gathered in an earthenware pitcher.

Slotted for each utensil and covered in Pacific cloth, these ready-made drawer liners are available at housewares stores.

The deep drawers in this vintage cabinet accommodate stacks of napkins without creasing a one.

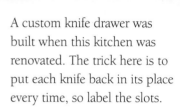

A custom knife drawer was built when this kitchen was renovated. The trick here is to put each knife back in its place every time, so label the slots.

Having drawers built specifically for your needs is a luxury. Proper planning ensures the right space for each piece.

TIP Lay out all of the cutlery that you want to fit into each drawer on a piece of sturdy brown paper. Draw a grid incorporating each group and be sure to allow for the longest pieces.

A drawer simply divided into three sections will work perfectly for six-piece place settings of silver if, like this one, it's long enough to accommodate two deep.

TIP To keep silverware from tarnishing, glue Pacific cloth to the bottom and sides of the drawer sections with nonsulfur glue. Purchase both cloth and glue at housewares stores.

You can easily make almost any standard drawer into a fitted silverware drawer by inserting ready-made drawer liners notched out for forks, knives, and spoons. Or try a less formal approach to keeping cutlery in place in your kitchen drawers. Choose from a variety of cutlery trays—wicker, wire, wood, or plastic—to make the best use of the space. Items infrequently used can be tied so they don't rattle around.

Leave your cutlery and cooking tools on the counter within easy reach in jars, jugs, or vases—anything that works with the style of your kitchen. For example, forks, knives, and spoons stored in antique pressed-glass celery vases on a dining room buffet look decorative while awaiting use.

This extra closet was converted into open shelving for a collection of tableware.

TIP A strip of molding, nailed near the back of each shelf and painted to match, keeps platters from sliding.

The antique corner cupboard is beautiful filled with a collection of blue-and-white spongeware, but it could just as easily house everyday china and glassware.

TIP Don't put your "good" china on the top shelf of your kitchen cabinets; the more difficult it is to reach, the less likely you are to use it.

A narrow cabinet has been transformed into a bar. Squeeze more space from a shelf by alternating glasses stem up and stem down.

Open shelving can take the form of a cabinet without a door, which leaves the glasses on view.

This frosted glass-front cabinet
with dentil crown molding is
set over a sideboard and used
exclusively for bar glasses.

OPPOSITE: A late-nineteenth-century painted cupboard serves the dual purpose of housing table linens and sound equipment conveniently near the dining table.

A glass-front cupboard adjacent to the dining room keeps table linens organized and in plain view.

TIP **It is most effective to collect linens in a single color, if you plan to display them in a glass-front storage piece.**

The upper part of an Empire cabinet hides linens for a sofa bed; table linens are kept underneath.

The Bar

There is something welcoming about a tray filled with bar paraphernalia: sparkling glasses, gleaming silver, crisp linen napkins. Whether half-hidden by a curtain, on a Deco bar cart, or on a side table, a well-stocked bar tray signals friends that you're ready to be hospitable.

1 On a pewter charger, antique apothecary bottles with ground-glass tops are filled with after-dinner drinks and dried fruit soaking in wine. Sometimes the storage solution is organization. By limiting the space for bar paraphernalia to a tray, you prevent it from spreading out and looking cluttered.

2 A long painted table in a country house is ready for any drinking preference. There is no need to search a cabinet for the obscure liquor Uncle Jake drinks; you can see a full bottle is present. When guests are expected, all that's needed is a bucket of ice and a tray of soft drinks.

3 The tea cart is making a comeback. A practical way to dedicate a space to all of your hosting needs, it can be easily wheeled into a room where you want to entertain or rolled out of the way.

TIP Tea carts can be put to work for a variety of storage needs. Don't limit yourself to beverages—use your imagination.

4 This inviting vignette was created in an alcove off the living room. Soft golden lighting behind the tieback curtains makes the silver on the bar look glamorous.

2

3 4

Benches We don't usually think of benches as

adding storage space, but, in fact, when stacked one on top of the other, they can.

There are probably as many styles of bookcases as there are books,

from very makeshift to very elegant. In the makeshift and instant gratification

category, my favorite is created by stacking up old country benches,

one on top of the other, until you have the shelf space needed.

1 Putting a small bench on top of a table increases usable surface space.

2 Stacked benches can even be arranged to minimize the impact of a video intercom.

3 Four unmatched old benches, stacked from the largest on bottom to the smallest on top, create a bookcase pyramid.

4 A pair of matching benches are stacked up to house a collection of miniature chairs.

5 Stack them by the front door and you have a place for keys and mail waiting to be sorted and read.

2 3

4 5

San Francisco party planner Stanlee Gatti houses 1940s Barbara Willis pottery in a blond vintage display cabinet with sliding glass doors.

Stereo speakers, camouflaged in an old wood lobster trap, are housed on the lower shelf of a side table.

CHAPTER III

Living Rooms, Dens, and Libraries

Living Room a sitting room for all-around use

Den a private retreat for work or pleasure

Cabinet a place for storing or displaying articles of value

Library a collection of books for reading, study, or reference

Modern living rooms have become what parlors were to our grandparents: formal rooms for receiving company. Those rooms for "living"—where we gather, relax, entertain—have moved to other parts of the house. Today's living rooms are seldom used for storage. The exceptions are books, sound systems, televisions, and the tapes and disks that accompany them. Sound systems usually fit in easily among books on open or closed shelves. The challenge is to house a bulky television in a piece of furniture that seamlessly blends with your room and still allows for comfortable viewing.

In apartments, where space is at a premium, living rooms do serve multiple ends. But houses often have a less formal room for everyday living. A den, library, or family room is that place—a room that serves so many purposes and catches so many elements of our lives that every inch of space in it has to count. A good solution is to dedicate the length of one wall to storage.

Start by making a list of everything that you want to house in the space: family photographs; kids' memorabilia; maps and travel books; archived periodicals; books; tapes and disks; board games; writing paper and art supplies. Then, decide whether you want to build in a unit or look for antique or new cupboards to fit your needs.

In this small living room with no built-in storage, baskets, boxes, and trunks double as furniture and storage.

A handsome wicker trunk can hide all sorts of things. Slip it out of the way under a glamorous credenza.

TIP Have a piece of glass or Plexiglas cut to the size of your trunk and let it stand in as a coffee table, housing items infrequently needed.

Baskets that slide out like drawers are used by designer Stephen Brady for archiving magazines. Though probably designed for a bedroom, this unit easily fits into a public room.

Here's the answer to the question of what to do with that big status gift box your fur throw came in: Fill it with videos and tuck it under the TV, where it's still subtly visible.

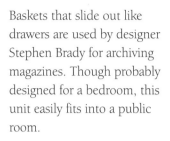

A great way to get extra storage dressed up enough for the living room is by making a skirt, either tailored or gathered, to cover a basic table. A glass top adds the finishing touch.
TIP You can add space by having the table made with a shelf or two.

Gift-wrap supplies are easy to
access in the traylike basket
and the shelf above.

You can make almost any old cupboard work for housing and hiding a TV by cutting a hole out of the back to allow room for the deepest part of the picture tube.

There's no reason why armoires, which are conventionally used in bedrooms, can't make an architectural contribution to a living space while providing much-needed storage.

With a beautiful basket, space on top of a wardrobe is put to use as an archive.

A big French provincial armoire has a solid shelf at just the right height for the TV and stereo components. The drawer below is ideal for tapes and disks.

A screen door barely hides the contents of this closet; therefore, it is used for a collection of vintage photographs.

TIP Using a pull-out swivel shelf for the TV in a closet allows you to watch from any seat in the room.

A corner cupboard does not usually have enough depth to hold a TV, but it can be retrofitted. Cut rectangular holes out of the back of the cupboard where the picture tube protrudes, leaving the center support untouched. The cupboard may need to stand out from the wall a little more than usual to allow for the TV back.

TIP Paint the inside of your cupboard a different color from the outside. It adds a finished look when the door is open.

Rather than push these two
cabinets up against each other,
two newlyweds separated
them to fill the wall space,
installed a rail and hung a
curtain between them, and
presto! A clever space for
mops and brooms.

One wall of this library/den is filled with closets built like cupboards with wide crown molding and vintage shutter doors. Because the closets stop 2 feet shy of the ceiling, they create the illusion of being furniture rather than a built-in unit. The extra space on top is ideal for storing and displaying a collection of toy trucks.

Each set of doors hides specific storage: a TV, sound equipment, tapes, and disks in one; shoe-box photograph storage in the next; periodicals and books in the rest.

Trunks used as coffee and side tables offer storage for out-of-season clothing and bedding.

It's essential to have a place to toss unread magazines and catalogs. This vintage basket is big enough to hold two stacks of magazines side by side.

TIP Get yourself a sturdy canvas bag just the right size for magazines, and put the newest ones in it. That way, whenever you go away for the weekend or want to climb into bed to read, you can just grab the bag and bring it with you.

This entire living-room wall, designed by architect Alan Buchsbaum, is devoted to multipurpose storage. Hidden behind a door when not in use, the TV is on a roll-out cart, so couch potatoes can view it from anywhere in the living room.

While not very practical, the Léger-inspired figure adds a note of whimsy, softening the severity of the grid. Many of the upper shelves were set aside to display a collection of pottery and cast-iron door-stops.

Buchsbaum designed drawers specifically for CDs.

Artist Chuck Close was one of the first to lean art on a shelf. When Close curated an exhibition at the Museum of Modern Art in New York City, he used this technique, even overlapping the works of famous artists, to create an informal and irreverent attitude. At home, too, the Closes have their art sitting on narrow shelves. "Mainly I did it because I didn't want to pound a nail into the wall. . . . I'm so indecisive." The result: living room as informal gallery.

A narrow shelf with a raised front edge allows you to constantly change artwork without committing a picture to one place forever.

When book editor Roy Finamore bought his Manhattan apartment, he didn't know where to house all of his books. His solution was to turn a second bedroom into a cozy dining room/library.

TIP Since your dining room is usually used only for dinner, double up its use by filling the walls with bookshelves.

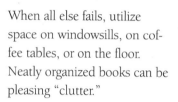

When all else fails, utilize space on windowsills, on coffee tables, or on the floor. Neatly organized books can be pleasing "clutter."

OPPOSITE: There are two reasons why this shelving looks so stylish: First, it is painted white. Second, the shelves are all at the same level, forming a graphic grid.

Avid collectors of books and records chose basic metal warehouse shelving for the entire wall of their SoHo loft. The library ladder slides along a metal rod, making access to the top shelves possible.

LEFT: If you have height, use it! In this narrow but soaring space in a SoHo loft, the shelving was boldly built to the ceiling. A classic library ladder, which slides on wheels and a brass rail, is a necessity.

TIP An angled shelf at eye height with a reading light above it is a great convenience.

A collection of spatterware jugs lives on the painted mantel—sometimes empty—but in springtime filled with hydrangeas.

Collections are rarely put away

out of view; they show off best when displayed

by color or design. Through our collections we enhance our lives and express our

personalities. The point is not to hide them behind closed doors

but to display them in either found spaces or specially created areas.

1 Tastes change, prescriptions change; sometimes we just buy multiple pairs of eyeglasses. Gather them together in a leather tray and presto!—a collection.

2 It is so natural for party planner Stanlee Gatti to create vignettes that he has even made his disposable lighters into a collection.

TIP When collecting a category, also collect by color for the most pulled-together look.

3 Why hide collectible boxes in a box? An old book defines the space allotted to this collection of horn boxes.

4 Collections don't have to contain things of great monetary value. Here a collection of mostly turn-of-the-century American enameled colanders is simply stacked on the kitchen counter and often used.

5 A collection of vintage Japanese pots in limited shapes and colors creates a cohesive look.

6 Sometimes a collection just happens. All of a sudden you find that you have six vintage wood bread boards, and a collection has started! Now you begin seeing and buying bread boards everywhere. Store them where you use them.

7 An extensive collection of vases made in Indiana in the early 1900s by Teco Potters fills the top of Robert Lee Morris's Stickley buffet.

1

2

3

4

5

6

7

Photographs are among our most precious possessions. Yet so often we hide them away in albums behind closed doors, thinking that means we are really organized. I like to take my cue from the art world and have a changing exhibit of photographs all the time. How do you hang art without making a commitment to a specific spot on the wall? One great answer is the exhibition ledge.

1, 3 A shelf mounted at the height at which you would conventionally hang art allows the collector to continually change the photographs without hammering into the wall.

TIP Have a groove cut into the shelf so that the frames don't slip.

2 Hardware store corner braces allow pictures simply to lean and almost float, giving them an interesting dimension.

4 What do you do with the newest family photographs? Try hanging a commercial postcard rack on a wall in the den or office. You can easily fit several packs of photos into each horizontal and vertical section.

5 Narrow shelves built into a niche have a front lip to keep framed photographs from sliding off.

6 Commercial angle irons are a really basic variation on the shelf. Stanlee Gatti displays his collection of 1930s flower oil paintings against the cast concrete walls of his workshop.

2

3 4

5

6

We built out the walls on either side of the French windows in our bedroom to create closets in the dead space under the pitched roof. As so often happens, the closets gave the room a more interesting shape.

CHAPTER IV

Bedrooms

Clothes Closet a recess off a room for storing clothes

Shoe Shelf a board fixed on a wall

Chest of Drawers a case in which drawers slide

Shirts, skirts, sweaters, pants, dresses, shoes, socks, handbags, jeans, T-shirts, underwear, coats, hats, gloves, jewelry—there are so many things to fit into our poor inadequate bedroom closets. Unless you are blessed with an extra room just for clothes—or unless you are monastic—you've probably had to resort to all sorts of alternative and makeshift receptacles to catch the overflow. Even if space is not an issue, organizing all that stuff undoubtedly is.

In this chapter, there are lots of tips: where to find space to build in closets or add a freestanding cupboard; how to fit an additional shelf or a stack of wire baskets into an existing closet; when and how to make a collection out of your favorite things, such as jewelry, sunglasses, or handbags, by displaying them instead of closeting them.

Oftentimes the answer to an overflowing closet is simply a serious spring cleaning. Here's how I clean out my clothes closet: First, like everyone else, I procrastinate until it's almost summer. Then I buy all new white plastic hangers (the heavy ones). Next I rent a portable garment rack and move everything from one rod at a time onto the rack. Then, one by one, I change the hangers for *everything*, which forces me to look at each piece of clothing and decide if I am really ever going to wear it again. I do the same thing with sweaters and shirts as I refold and assess each one. At the end of the process, which could take days, I have a gorgeously tidy closet with space to fill up again and bundles of usable clothes for the thrift shop.

On one side we put shelves for everything from a stereo to sweatpants.

TIP Wire shelves utilize space more efficiently than any other drawers or shelving, and you can buy them in a variety of sizes.

On the other side we put in double-hung rods for shirts and pants.

TIP Always put a shelf over closet rods for additional storage.

Because you can see everything inside at a glance, a vintage glass-front library cabinet makes an excellent clothing storage unit. You can still buy cabinets like this one at relatively reasonable prices at both city and rural flea markets.

Architect David Mann installed this thoroughly modern storage system in a niche of adman Jeff McKay's compact New York City apartment. He used industrial steel shelves and brackets—the kind used in restaurant kitchens—to hold galvanized boxes for folded clothes. Clothes are hung from aluminum hangers on a basic portable garment rack. The trick: a limited palate, a very good memory, and a superneat aesthetic.

You have to duck through the Alice in Wonderland door into this great long closet, located under the pitched eaves of the house. Unlike random attic storage, rods provide a tidy place to hang pants and shirts, and shelves hold folded things, leaving plenty of room for shoes and satchels.

TIP Always leave enough space between the bottom of hanging clothes and the floor for shoes.

An overcounter cupboard seems like an odd place for shoes, but it puts them at eye level, so you can know at a glance if your heels are worn-down.

TIP Things don't always have to be stored in traditional places: look up, look down, look under.

LEFT: A narrow cupboard in a summerhouse bedroom is filled with storage boxes, all labeled for easy access. **TIP For added storage, find an odd cupboard to fill the space between windows.**

OPPOSITE: If your guest bed-room is short on closet space, you can simply retrofit an antique cupboard with a wood rod for hangers and a shelf or two for extra bedding. Add a couple of rows of hooks for quick hang-ups and benches for stacking books and magazines.

Architect Alan Buchsbaum designed this elegant walk-in clothes closet for New Yorkers Allan and Pat Dennis. Without really building a separate room, he defined the closet space with custom cabinets reminiscent of 1920s steamer trunks.

TIP **You could create a similar feeling by using folding screens to define the space and placing a vintage trunk in front for storage.**

Vintage shutters were used as doors on a pair of small cupboardlike closets built on either side of a daybed, creating a cozy niche for reading and essential storage.

In one closet there is a rod for hanging clothes; on the other side are shelves for bed linens.

TIP Crown molding around the top of the boxlike closets gives them the look and feel of freestanding furniture while maintaining the shape of the room.

You can create an entry in a small rectangular bedroom by building in boxlike closets in the corners. This not only solves the storage problem but also makes the room more private and interesting.

Fit out one side with rods for double-hung clothes and the other with shelves for a TV and folded clothes.

TIP **By not building the closets up to the ceiling, you visually maintain the room's original size and sense of space.**

Next to the bed, under the
night table, a big basket is
filled with bedtime reading,
leaving table space free.

For years, we looked for dressers of the right dimensions and colors. Finally, we gave up and built "garages" under the windows in two bedroom dormers. The top shelf was doubled in thickness and the edge bullnosed to add the look of finished furniture. A simple middle shelf was set back about 2 inches so as not to interrupt the fall of the curtain. A 1¾-inch wood curtain rod holds the slightly gathered curtain.

TIP **If you always keep your traveling bags half packed and ready to go, you can easily slip them out of view behind the curtain.**

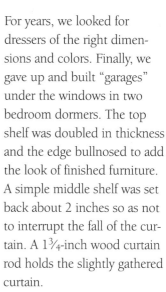

TIES

What could be more perfect
for a vintage tie collection than
a vintage 1930s men's
wardrobe? There are brass
labels for everything so that
author Peter Biskind won't put
his clothing in the wrong
place.

132

A set of very simple shelves was built to surround a bed, almost as a headboard, with space for water, nighttime reading, and display doubling as a headboard.

More ideas for hooks. Here, Victorian hooks with porcelain knobs were screwed in behind the bedroom door.

Not all pegboards need be vintage. This was made with scraps of wood and dowel and painted to match.

Closets everywhere: in the hall, along the wall, and facing the bed, designed for both hanging space and drawers.

In this newly renovated bedroom, closets were built out from the wall and shelves built into the sides. The bed nestles in between, with wall becoming headboard and shelves at the ready for evening neccessities.

New hooks were attached to the mirror frame for an instant hat rack.

In this newly renovated garden apartment, a wall of glossy laminated panels—with no visible hardware—hides it all, from T-shirts and socks to the stereo. Hanging storage is in a walk-in closet.

Stereo equipment lives comfortably behind the panel cut to accommodate the stairs to the garden.

Panels pop open to reveal simple shelves and drawers.

The double rods in the walk-in are designed so the top rod isn't too high to reach. At the back of the closet is a 1970s display case from a shoe store; the glass sections clip together.

TIP Hunt flea markets for unusual shoe storage systems.

Hooks and Pegs are handy

things to have around. A hook in a strategic spot makes it faster and easier to keep your clothes off the table, chair, or floor.

1 A row of Shaker-style pegs on a board easily screws into the wall of a bathroom, ready to catch bracelets, necklaces, antique baskets, and candles.

TIP You can order wood Shaker reproduction peg boards by mail through Shaker gift shops. Use them unpainted or paint to match your wall, as in this bathroom.

2 This vintage hook board with its original paint is used for bathrobes and towels.

3 Place hooks at different heights for a variety of uses.

4 Vintage hook boards make great hanging spaces in a guest bedroom.

TIP Hanging two hook boards one over the other doubles the hanging space. The lower one is ideal for kid guests.

5 Keep your eyes open for unusual old metal hooks at flea markets.

6 A freestanding coatrack is cute and practical for a child's room.

7 You can make a hook board by simply cutting a length of 1 × 3-inch lumber to the size you want and screwing on old or new hooks. The beaded edge can be routed by a carpenter or at the lumberyard and adds a nice finish.

TIP You are less likely to crack or chip your wall if you screw a board into the wall and the hooks into the board.

8 In this small bathroom, a conveniently placed hook board holds not only towels but rolls of toilet paper.

2 3

4

5

6

7

8

Bathroom necessities peek out from diamond-shaped cutouts on the doors of this bathroom closet.

CHAPTER V

Bathrooms

Medicine Chest a chest for keeping a select set of medicines

Makeup the articles used for painting one's face, especially cosmetics

Shelf a thin slab of wood fixed horizontally to a wall

We have one friend who loves to look into other people's medicine cabinets. She makes no bones about it, saying it speaks volumes about who people really are. Although most of us wouldn't have the nerve to come right out and say that we snoop, curiosity lurks.

Personally, I like a woman's bathroom to look somewhat glamorous and a man's bathroom to look handsome. I like to see beautiful bottles of cologne, silver-topped glass bottles, and silver or horn cups filled with makeup brushes and pencils. What I don't want to see are boxes of personal hygiene products or vials of medicine. There are a few tricks to arranging and organizing bathroom paraphernalia that will make any guest who uses your bathroom and dares to sneak a peek think you are the healthiest and neatest person in town.

The first thing to do is to buy yourself covered baskets in a variety of sizes. Woven wood picnic baskets, vintage or new, are great for toiletries that you want to keep out of sight, yet conveniently on hand. A smaller good-looking covered basket or box near your makeup mirror is the place to throw those unattractive cards of pills and tubes of creams—things you use every day that don't fit into any category and refuse to stack or stand up in your medicine chest.

A well-maintained medicine cabinet is the most crucial space of all. The trick here is to keep weeding out out-of-date makeup, medicine, unguents, and potions.

A wide windowsill makes a great shelf for antique pressed- and cut-glass bottles and jars originally used on Victorian dressing tables. Fill these bottles with useful everyday items like makeup pencils and brushes, toothbrushes, and razors.

TIP Transfer mouthwash from the large ugly plastic bottle it comes in to a small elegant decanter.

A man's collection of bathroom necessities can be as attractive as a woman's. Lucky guys—they don't need as much stuff, hence, less clutter.

TIP A flat woven basket tray makes a handsome, masculine container for toiletries.

The noted makeup artist Bobbi Brown's bathroom counter is pleasingly cluttered with her famous makeup arranged in silver julep cups and glass trays. **TIP Simply using silver cups to hold brushes, pencils, and flowers adds a touch of glamour. It's organization with style.**

An antique pie safe with refurbished screening fills a bathroom corner with character and at the same time offers an airy storage place for towels and soaps.

TIP To make your bathroom more like other rooms, fill any niche with odd or old pieces of furniture in which you can store necessities.

This antique cupboard, which just fit under the roofline, holds tons of bedroom and bathroom stuff.

TIP Store bottled water for bedside drinking conveniently in your bathroom instead of the kitchen.

This niche was not treated as a closet with a full set of doors. The bottom is a cupboard for hiding necessities; the top contains open shelves for towels.

Instead of building shelving all the way across this bathroom wall, narrow shelves provide compact storage and leave a niche for towel rods. The bright blue contrasting with white towels creates a visual treat.

TIP Sometimes smaller is better.

Skinny closets were built around this bathroom sink. On one side the narrowest wire shelves available provide the perfect place for socks and underwear. The other side has typical built-in shelves for towels, a hamper, and miscellaneous things.

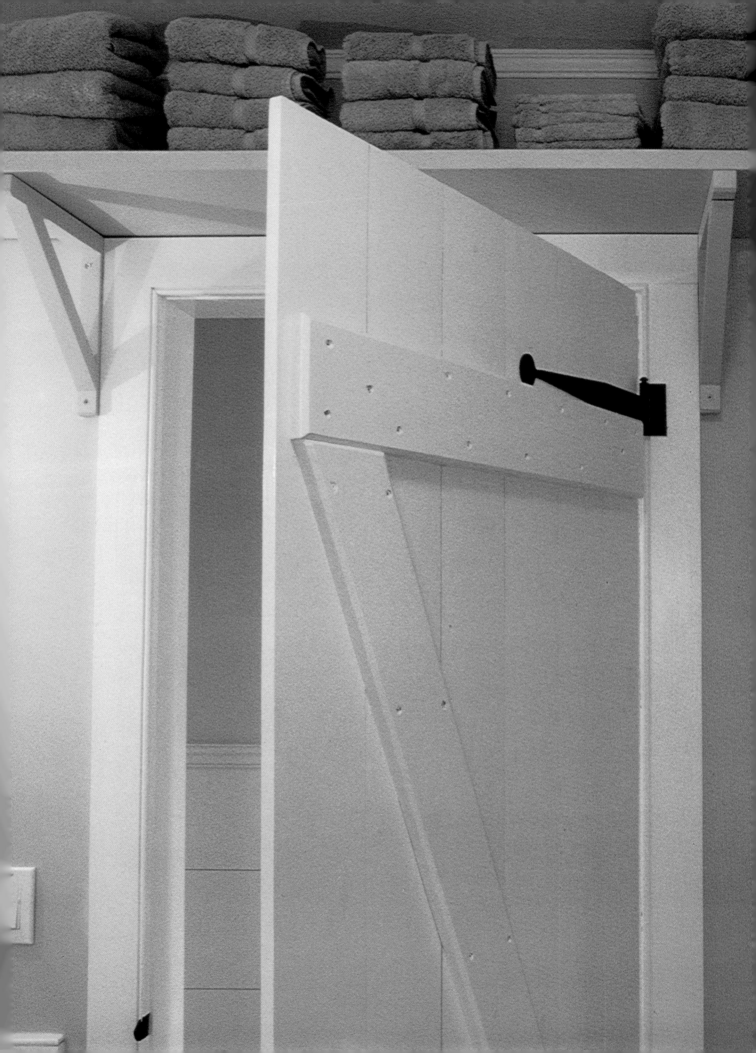

If there is space above your bathroom door, build a simple shelf to hold extra towels.

TIP Keeping extra towels in the bathroom, where they are used, saves space in the linen closet and avoids the bother of moving them from the closet to the bathroom.

The very narrow shelves in this bathroom closet are designed so small bottles, vials, tubes, and the like are all easy to spot and reach.

TIP Think big. When you are designing a new bathroom, opt for the maximum amount of storage space.

These towel hooks are the ultimate in modern discretion.

You can make almost any wood-framed mirror into a medicine cabinet. This antique gilded mirror is in fact the front of a medicine cabinet. An additional mirror on the inside of the door is great for putting on makeup.

TIP Have a cabinetmaker build a wood box the size of the inside measurements of the mirror frame. The outside dimension of the frame should be larger than the box so that the box is hidden behind the frame. Add adjustable glass shelves, screw the box to the wall, and hinge the frame onto the box.

If you prefer a clean and modern approach, try a ready-made beveled-edge medicine cabinet without a frame. A mirror and glass shop can make a simple aluminum frame to any size. Not only is this one very tall, but the recessed cabinet is unusually deep to hold tons of stuff.

TIP If you have the depth, make your cabinet deeper than standard.

Two is definitely better than one when it comes to couples sharing a bathroom and a medicine cabinet.
TIP If you don't have to share a medicine cabinet, don't.

If you're building or renovating, plan on recessing your medicine cabinet into the wall so that only the frame is exposed.

BOTTOM: Placed in a narrow space between two architectural windows, this reproduction farmhouse medicine cabinet is the only storage in the small bathroom.

Get a big handsome basket and fill it with rolls of toilet paper. You will never again have to worry about refilling those silly little rollers, and you get to avoid arguments about installing a roll "over" or "under." Plus, it's clear when a trip to the store for restocking is needed.

Colorful pails store tub toys in this child's bathroom.

OPPOSITE: You can use covered hampers and trunk-style baskets to conveniently hide personal hygiene products.

Laundry Rooms The laundry room is often the place where all clutter eventually lands, so it is a good idea to plan for a variety of storage: shelves for bed linens and towels, hooks for hangers, baskets for dirty clothes, benches for stacking and folding.

Even if space is limited, look high, look low, look up, look under. Make every inch count.

1 A new laundry room looks like a chick without feathers; the clutter hasn't arrived yet. The sturdy shelf along the entire back wall is a necessity.

2 To hide plugs and hoses, we made heavy curtains to hang from the shelf to the top of the washer and dryer. Big brass grommets in the canvas slide over hooks that are screwed into the underside of the shelf. It's a fun place to pin mementos, photos, and invitations.

3 Sturdy wood shelves are fitted into a deep niche and hold stacks of household linens. The absence of doors makes everything on the shelves easy to reach and easy to find.

4 An unheated storage room off the laundry room is accessible through a very low door. The screen window allows ventilation between the two rooms and provides a whimsical view.

5 Outside the laundry an odd chest of drawers, a wood trunk, and wicker hampers are filled with blocks of cedar to keep moths away from sweaters and wool blankets.

Baskets are not only one of man's earliest crafts but also one of the most useful creations for organizing all the by-products of modern civilization, the accumulation of stuff. Hatboxes and shoe boxes make good and good-looking storage for hats, scarves, gloves, and party shoes.

1 One favorite use for big beautiful baskets is holding stacks of fresh towels.

2 Keep all of your small travel bags and tags together in one handsome rectangular basket.

3 A huge sturdy basket that was used in the early 1900s for shipping goods makes an ideal container for storing a month's supply of table water, especially when it can slide under the kitchen worktable. Another basket holds spare bottles of wine.

4, 7 The favorite place in our house to keep the supply of toilet paper is in big baskets right next to each john.

5 A basket makes a convenient catchall for casual shoes.

6 The big closet-cleaning day always includes emptying all baskets and washing them under a warm running shower to get out the dust. Set them to dry outside in the sunshine or on a cotton rug in your bathroom.

8 If you want to hide your stereo speakers, put them in loosely woven baskets.

TIP Use open-weave baskets for camouflaging speakers on top of cupboards and armoires.

Since you supply the wood base, a log holder from the hardware store can be made to any length to fit your space. It keeps the wood off the damp ground and makes it easy to stack neatly.

CHAPTER VI

Sheds and Basements

Toolshed a structure, often open-fronted, for storing or sheltering tools

Basement the lowest story of a building beneath the principal one

Garage a building where motor vehicles are housed or tended

Basements, attics, garages, and toolsheds are a sort

of never-never land. Here lives the out-of-sight, out-of-mind stuff that we will probably never, ever want again. Think about it: How many garages are so filled to the brim that passengers have to get out of the car before it is pulled in?

Organizing a messy garage, barn, or basement into an orderly work space takes the same discipline as organizing the kitchen; however, it is much easier to put off. The first step is to be ruthless. Pull everything out into the middle of the space (if there is still a middle) or into the driveway and sort through it all. Then decide what you really could do without.

What do you do with the treasures you no longer need or want? Remember, "one man's junk is another man's treasure." Have a garage sale, tag sale, barn sale, yard sale—sell everything! Ask a quarter even when you think most things are worth at least $75! Ask a few energetic friends to help and trade them your old stuff for their effort. Then sweep out the spiderwebs and start from scratch.

Put up new nails and hooks for everything that has a handle, a strap, or a loop. Build simple wood shelves between the joists using hardware-store corner braces. Nail baskets into the walls to catch small things. Give each tool a place and always put it back in its place.

The process may be hard to start, but it's very cathartic. You're likely to feel really great when it's done!

It's not fancy, but this barn space is simply and practically organized with the use of the most utilitarian and basic lumberyard shelves, hooks, and nails. Apply the same principles to organizing your garage or basement.

All of the rakes, brooms, and galvanized tubs are hung from large galvanized nails on simple horizontal boards.

Hanging bicycles from the rafters not only keeps them out of the way but also preserves the tire rubber.

Each small tool has its own place.

TIP **When there is a place for each tool, it is much easier to remember to replace it and find it.**

Unfinished pine boards make quick, straightforward shelves.

TIP **If you install narrow shelves at eye level, everything will be easier to find.**

"Instant gratification" shelving is accomplished in a cement basement with no nailing or screwing by using cement blocks with 2 × 8-inch boards for shelves. Each glass jar is filled with only one size of nail or screw. Charley Gold's collection of coffee cans actually works well for odd hardware.

Cement blocks and 2 × 8-inch boards make fine shelving for wine storage in a cool basement. Wood wine crates keep the wine bottles separated by variety.

For simple tool storage in a cement-walled basement, strips of 1 × 3-inch lumber were nailed vertically into the wood header. Lengths of 1 × 6-inch lumber—with nails for everything from thermometers to extension cords to saws— are attached to the verticals.

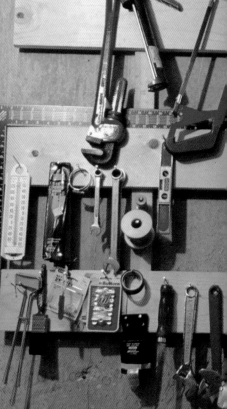

This simple outbuilding, probably built in the 1800s, was converted into a charming and orderly toolshed. The table and chairs add a romantic note and provide a work surface.

Our neighbors David and Liza built an attractive wall of continuous sheds along the side of their house to hide some of the uglier necessities in life, such as air-conditioning units and garbage cans. They also added a storage shed for baby Luc's toys. The trellis along the top of the plank doors and the vines soften the entire wall.

We built an enclosure for our outdoor shower and planted one little grapevine. Two years later we strung wires for the vines to follow, making a summer ceiling of hanging bunches of green grapes.

TIP If you want to enhance your shed, plant a fast-growing vine. String green wire in the direction in which you want the vine to grow.

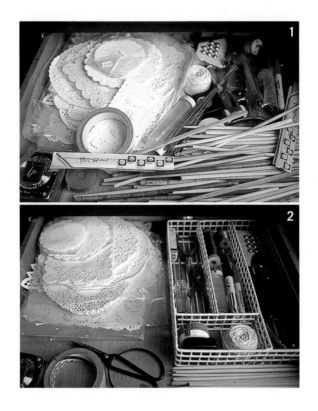

Before and After It's fun to start with a totally empty closet, cabinet, or drawer and determine what storage function it will serve best. Even more satisfying is making sense of the "junk drawer."

1, 2 A simple solution to the jumbled drawer. Using a wire-coated cutlery basket for all of the tools left a slot for chopsticks, plus enough space for pastry doilies and a few large items.

3, 4 An old green painted cupboard in a guest room is best suited to becoming a linen closet. But before you fill it, line the unpainted wood shelves with paper or fabric drawer liner for a clean, fresh finish.

5, 6 As is often the case, this kitchen drawer was a mess, with matchboxes and corkscrews and who-knows-what just thrown in. The solution: plastic dividers that snap off to the size of the drawer and clip together to form a grid, containing each category in its own compartment.

3 5

4

6

Resources

This directory will help you locate or reproduce most of the storage items shown throughout this book. Whether these items are antique, old, custom-made, industrial, or very common hardware store supplies, almost everything can be bought or duplicated.

If you are simply overwhelmed and need help organizing your office, clothes closets, kitchen pantry, or anything else, a professional organizer is a great investment. He or she will even orchestrate a major move. For the names of organizers in your area, call The National Association of Professional Organizers at 512-206-0151 (www.napo.net.com).

Baskets

Basketville

Consolidated Plastics Co., Inc.

Get Organized

Hold Everything

The Holding Company

Restoration Hardware

Williams-Sonoma

Boxes

Photo boxes, letter boxes, collection boxes, and all kinds of boxes for storage.

Exposures

Hold Everything

Closet Builders

California Closets

New York Closet Company

Poliform USA

Clothes Closet Accessories

Check out closet and house-wares stores in your neighborhood that carry hangers, tie racks, shoe storage, and cedar chips, or call for the following catalogs.

Get Organized

Hold Everything

Home Decorators Collection

Drawer Dividers

Local housewares and hardware stores all sell dividers.

Get Organized

Hold Everything

File Cabinets and Storage

Check your local stationery supply stores for new and used file cabinets.

Basketville

Hold Everything

Home Decorators Collection

Knoll

Pottery Barn

Staples

Hooks and Peg Hooks

Shop at flea markets, tag sales, antique shops, and local hardware stores.

Chambers

Hold Everything

Home Decorators Collection

Restoration Hardware

Shaker Workshops

Metro Shelving

Check your local Yellow Pages under "Shelving" for distributors near you. The following sources will provide metro shelving to order.

Ad Hoc Softwares

Hold Everything

Photo Exhibition Ledges

You can buy molding at your local lumberyard to fabricate your own; these sources offer standard sizes.

Hold Everything

Home Decorators
 Collection

Pottery Barn

Plastic Containers

Try your local housewares and grocery stores.

Consolidated Plastic Co.

Get Organized

Pot Stands

Look in flea markets and antique shops for vintage iron pot stands.

You can order reproductions in a variety of sizes and metals from the following source.

Williams-Sonoma

Screening

Your local hardware store will sell standard screening; the following will ship wire cloth in brass, bronze, copper, and stainless.

F. P. Smith Wire Cloth Co.

Spice Storage

The following catalogs feature steel and glass test-tube spice racks and wood drawer and door storage.

Dean & DeLuca

Williams-Sonoma

Stackable Shelving

Stackable shelving components in a variety of materials are available from the following sources.

Get Organized

Hold Everything

Pottery Barn

Storage Furniture

For old armoires, cupboards, medicine cabinets, and trunks, scour flea markets and antique stores; for new versions, try the following catalogs.

Chambers

Gardeners Eden

Hold Everything

Home Decorators
 Collection

Pottery Barn

Wire Basket Shelving

Shop at your local closet and housewares stores for wire shelving and basket components that best fit your space.

FURTHER INFORMATION

Ad Hoc Softwares

For store location:

212-925-2652

www.adhocny@aol.com

Basketville

Basket number N33HH will hold hanging files.

For retail store locations:

802-387-5509

www.basketville.com

California Closets

To order a catalog or for
    store locations:

1-800-274-6754

Chambers

To order a catalog:

1-800-334-1254

Consolidated Plastics Co., Inc.

Industrial-type storage, sold by the case only.

To order a catalog:

1-800-362-1000

330-425-3333 (fax)

Dean & DeLuca

To order a catalog:

1-800-221-7714

1-800-781-4050 (fax)

www.dean-deluca.com

Exposures

To order a catalog or for
    store locations:

1-800-222-4947

F. P. Smith Wire Cloth Co.

To order a catalog:

1-800-323-6842

www.fpsmith.com

Gardeners Eden

To order a catalog or for
    store locations:

1-800-822-9600

Get Organized

To order a catalog:

1-800-803-9400

Hold Everything

To order a catalog or for
    store locations:

1-800-421-2264

www.holdeverything.com

The Holding Company

For store locations in
    London:

011 171 610 9160

www.theholdingcom
    pany.co.uk

Home Decorators Collection

To order a catalog:

1-800-245-2217

314-521-5780 (fax)

Knoll

For information and a cata-
    log on Calibre vertical
    file components:

1-800-445-5045

www.knoll.com

New York Closet Company

For store locations:

212-439-9500

Poliform USA

To order a catalog or for
store locations:

1-888-Poliform (catalog)

www.poliform.usa.com

Pottery Barn

To order a catalog or for
store locations:

1-800-922-5507

www.potterybarn.com

Restoration Hardware

To order a catalog or for
store locations:

1-800-762-1005

415-927-9690 (fax)

www.restorationhard
ware.com

Shaker Workshops

To order a catalog:

1-800-840-9121

www.shakerworkshop.
com

Williams-Sonoma

To order a catalog or for
store locations:

1-800-541-2233

www.williamssonoma.com

Index